40 Days of Hope in Grief and Loss

Finding Strength and Encouragement Daily Devotional

Mike Prah

Mpaebo Media
We Make It Happen

Mpaebo Media

Copyright © 2025 by Mike Prah

Published by Mpaebo Media, a division of Mike Prah, LLC, Severn, MD. www.mikeprah.com

All rights reserved solely by the author. No portion of this book may be reproduced in any form or by any means, except for brief quotations, without the written permission of the author.

Due to the evolving nature of the Internet, any web addresses, links, or URLs provided in this publication are subject to change or deletion and may no longer be available. The author and publisher assume no responsibility for such an occurrence.

Scripture quotations taken from the Holy Bible, New International Version (NIV). Copyright © 1973, 1978, 1984, 2011 by Biblica, Inc.™. Used by permission. All rights reserved.

Scripture quotations taken from the Holy Bible, New Living Translation (NLT). Copyright ©1996, 2004, 2007 by Tyndale House Foundation. Used by permission of Tyndale House Publishers, Inc.

Scripture quotations taken from The Message (MSG). Copyright © 1993, 1994, 1995, 1996, 2000, 2001, 2002. Used by permission of NavPress Publishing Group. Used by permission. All rights reserved.

Scripture quotations taken from the Berean Standard Bible (BSB) –Public Domain.

Scripture quotations taken from the Contemporary English Version (CEV). Copyright © 1995 American Bible Society. Used by permission. All rights reserved.

Italics in Scripture reflect the author's added emphasis.

U. S. LIBRARY OF CONGRESS CATALOGING-IN-PUBLICATION DATA

Name: Prah, Mike, author

Title: 40 Days of Hope in Grief and Loss: Finding Strength and Encouragement Daily Devotional | Mike Prah

Description: Maryland, [2025] | Includes bibliographical references

Identifiers: LCCN: 20250822_162708 | ISBN: 979-8-9906475-3-4 (Hardcover) | ISBN: 979-8-9906475-7-2 (ebook)

40 DAYS OF HOPE IN GRIEF AND LOSS

Classification: LCC BKRHJJ-X3

First Edition

Special Bulk Discounts and Custom Editions:

Most books authored by Mike Prah are available at special discounted rates for bulk purchases by churches, organizations, businesses, and individuals. Customized editions or book excerpts can also be created to meet the specific needs of your ministry, event, or audience. For more information or to inquire about a special order, please contact: **info@mikeprah.com**

Praise for 40 Days of Hope in Grief and Loss

IN TIMES OF GRIEF AND LOSS, we often feel vulnerable, asking questions like, "Where is God?" "Why did this happen?" or "Is the Lord truly among His people?" Yet take heart: *"The Lord already knew what He was going to do"* (John 6:6). God is never surprised, never powerless, and He promises to walk with us, never leaving nor forsaking us.

Jesus, our compassionate High Priest, understands our pain, empathizes with our struggles, and offers true comfort. He knows how to walk with you and lead you through.

In this timely book, Pastor Mike Prah offers biblical wisdom and heartfelt guidance to help you face grief with faith, hope, and strength. Whether you are grieving now or preparing for future trials, you'll find perspective and encouragement to navigate loss with confidence in God's presence and purpose.

—**PASTOR DR. CALEB OWUSU ADU**, Overseer, Spring City Church, Church of Pentecost International

My friend, Pastor Mike Prah, has given the Body of Christ a timely gift with *40 Days of Hope in Grief and Loss*. This devotional does not minimize the pain of sorrow or offer quick fixes; instead, it serves as a tender companion for the heart that is hurting with daily applications, reflections, and prayer. From Day 1—God Sees Your Tears to Day 40—A Life Well Finished, the readings are rooted in the timeless truths of Scripture, reminding us that God not only sees our tears but holds them close, and that His presence remains our anchor even when life feels overwhelming.

Through Scripture, reflection, and stories of others who have walked the valley of loss, Pastor Prah gently points us back to the God of all comfort who promises to never leave us alone in our grief. What sets this devotional apart is its honesty; it makes room for brokenness, questions, and slow steps forward, while consistently offering hope through Jesus Christ.

Whether you are mourning the loss of a loved one, a dream, or a season of life, these 40 days will remind you that healing is not about forgetting but about remembering with faith, grieving with hope, and trusting the One who makes all things new. This is a resource I highly recommend to anyone walking through the sacred journey of grief.

—**BISHOP GEORGE W. HAWKINGS JR.**, Sr Pastor, High Calling Ministries and Washington MetropolitanDistrict Bishop, Ark United

Christian Community Churches International (AUCCCI)

Hebrews 4:15 reminds us, *"For we have not ahigh priest which cannot be touched with the feeling of our infirmities..."* In the same way, we are blessed with a pastor and author who is not untouched by sorrow and grief. Thankfully, God does not leave us in a state of grief and loss—He gently leads us toward an often elusive outcome of our pain—hope.

In *40 Days of Hope in Grief and Loss,* Mike Prah masterfully shows that hope is not absent in grief—it is present, patiently waiting to be discovered. Through his compassionate and Spirit-led words, we are guided toward that light. Thank you, Pastor Mike, for helping us see that even in the valley, hope remains.

— PASTOR EMERITUS TL ROGERS, Founder, The Triumphant Church and Emerging Pastors Network

In life's wilderness seasons—when sorrow floods the soul and loss shakes our foundation—*40 Days of Hope in Grief and Loss* offers a gentle, Scripture-rich companion for the journey. With a pastor's warmth and wisdom of God's Word, Pastor Mike Prah invites readers to encounter Jesus where the tears fall, and rise again in Hope, be restored by Grace, and held by Mercy.

Rooted in his life's mission to introduce people to Christ and equip them to live out their God-given purpose, Pastor

Prah offers daily encouragement that points beyond pain to a Person—Jesus.

This devotional helps readers grow in Christ, trust God's timing, and embrace the mission to glorify Him—even in suffering. Each page breathes the prayerful blessing of Romans 15:13: *"May the God of hope fill you with all joy and peace as you trust in him, so that you may overflow with hope by the power of the Holy Spirit."*

Keep this devotional close in your personal walk and give another copy to someone navigating loss. Let's be like Christ and live as His church—receiving Hope, Grace, and Mercy, then offering them freely to a hurting world. As Scripture reminds us: *"[God] comforts us in all our troubles, so that we can comfort those in any trouble with the comfort we ourselves receive from* God" —2 Corinthians 1:4 (NIV).

—DR. CHRISTOPHER KUIPER, STRATEGIC LEADER, FINANCE PROFESSIONAL, UNIVERSITY PROFESSOR

Contents

Introduction	XII
1. God Sees Your Tears	1
2. Held in God's Hands	3
3. God Is Your Safe Place	5
4. God Is Close to the Brokenhearted	7
5. When Words Fall Short, God Still Hears	9
6. A Song in the Night	11
7. Hope in the Valley of Trouble	13
8. The Gift of God's Comfort	15
9. The Hope That Anchors	17
10. Worship Through the Tears	19

11.	Never Separated	21
12.	You Are Not Alone	23
13.	The Last Word Belongs to Victory	25
14.	Held in His Hand	27
15.	No More Tears	29
16.	Strength in the Midst of Sorrow	31
17.	Peace in the Middle of Pain	33
18.	Through the Waters and Flames	35
19.	Waiting with Hope	37
20.	Death Is Not the End	39
21.	You Are Not Alone	41
22.	Life Beyond the Grave	43
23.	Christ Defeated Death	45
24.	Rest for the Weary Heart	47
25.	Joy Will Come Again	49
26.	When Life Knocks You Down	51
27.	Understanding Will Come Later	53
28.	Still Standing	55
29.	Their Work Will Follow Them	57

30.	Comforted to Comfort Others	59
31.	Because He Lives	61
32.	A Promise You Can Count On	63
33.	A Reunion is Coming	65
34.	We Belong to the Lord	67
35.	Light Trouble, Eternal Glory	69
36.	Eyes on the Unseen	71
37.	We Do Not Grieve Without Hope	73
38.	Comforted By the Coming of the Lord	75
39.	The Gain of Eternal Life	77
40.	A Life Well Finished	79
	Endnotes	83
	Other Books By Mike Prah	86
	Connect with Mike Prah	92

Introduction

"… I WILL TRANSFORM THE VALLEY OF TROUBLE INTO A GATEWAY OF HOPE" HOSEA 2:15 (NLT)

Grief touches every soul. Whether sudden or prolonged, grief leaves a mark that no words can erase. It is a sacred wound—a reminder of deep love and irreplaceable loss. In the shadows of pain, we often feel disoriented, wondering if joy will ever return or if we'll ever feel "normal" again.

This devotional is not a roadmap out of grief, but a companion on the journey through it. *40 Days of Hope in Grief and Loss* offers daily encouragement drawn from the timeless truths of God's Word. Each devotion gently points you to the heart of God, who not only sees your tears but gathers them, who not only hears your cries but draws near to comfort you (Psalm 56:8; Isaiah 41:10).

In these 40 days, you'll be reminded of the enduring hope found in Jesus Christ. You'll find stories of others who've walked through the valley of sorrow and encountered the sustaining grace of God. You'll encounter scriptures that speak directly to the pain of loss while offering peace, strength, and assurance.

Whether you are grieving the loss of a loved one, a relationship, a dream, or even a season of life that's passed, this journey is for you. It's okay to feel broken, to ask hard questions, and to move slowly. God doesn't rush your healing—He walks with you through it. His presence is your anchor. His promises are your hope.

As you walk through these 40 days, may you sense that you're not alone. The God of all comfort is beside you, ahead of you, and holding you. Each devotion is a gentle reminder that healing doesn't mean forgetting. It means remembering with faith, grieving with hope, and trusting the One who promises to make all things new.

Prayer for the Journey

Heavenly Father, I lift every heart that picks up this book in search of comfort and hope. Lord, You are close to the brokenhearted and near to those crushed in spirit. May Your presence be felt in every moment of sorrow and silence. Bring peace that surpasses understanding, strength that endures the storms, and hope that anchors weary souls.

Comfort each reader in their unique journey through loss. Remind them that their pain is seen, their tears are precious to You, and their story is not over. May Your love be the light in their darkest nights and Your Word the balm for their aching hearts.

In every devotion, speak truth. In every Scripture, breathe life. In every prayer, restore trust in Your goodness and Your promise never to leave or forsake us.

I surrender every reader's grief to You, our Healer and Redeemer, as we wait in expectation for the joy, peace, and comfort You promise to bring. *In Jesus' Name, Amen.*

Mike Prah

"I will ... transform the Valley of Trouble into a gateway of hope."

— Hosea 2:15 (NLT)

One

God Sees Your Tears

"You keep track of all my sorrows. You have collected all my tears in your bottle. You have recorded each one in your book." — Psalm 56:8 (NLT)

When author C.S. Lewis lost his beloved wife, Joy, to cancer, he poured out his sorrow in a journal that became the book *A Grief Observed*. He confessed, "No one ever told me that grief felt so like fear."[1] His honesty reminds us that even great faith does not shield us from sorrow, but it does give us a place to bring our tears.

Grief is a journey often walked in silence. In the lonely spaces where no one else sees the pain, but God sees us. Psalm 56:8 reveals a comforting truth—God doesn't dismiss our tears. He records them. He keeps them. He cares deeply about every drop that falls from our eyes.

The Bible doesn't shy away from emotion. Job cried out. David wept. Jesus Himself sobbed at the tomb of Lazarus. Our tears are not weaknesses to be hidden, but offerings to be held by God. Grief may be loud and unpredictable or quiet and persistent, but in every form, it matters to God.

You do not need to explain your grief or try to be strong. God is close to the brokenhearted (Psalm 34:18), and He promises to heal the wounds that time cannot heal. When the ache returns uninvited or the silence grows louder, remember, God has not forgotten you or your pain. He bottles every tear.

Practical Application:

Take a few minutes today to share your grief with God. Be honest. Let it all out. Then read Psalm 56:8 again and imagine Him holding those words, just as He holds your tears—with tenderness and care.

Reflection:

How does knowing that God keeps track of every tear change the way you view your grief?

Prayer:

God, You see me when I cry. You care about every sorrow I carry. Help me to trust that my pain is not wasted and that You are walking with me through this valley. Thank You for holding my tears and holding my heart. In Jesus' name, Amen.

Read More: Revelation 21:4; Psalm 34:18; Isaiah 53:3–4; John 11:35; Romans 8:26

Two

Held in God's Hands

> "I GIVE THEM ETERNAL LIFE, AND THEY WILL NEVER PERISH. NO ONE CAN SNATCH THEM AWAY FROM ME, FOR MY FATHER HAS GIVEN THEM TO ME, AND HE IS MORE POWERFUL THAN ANYONE ELSE. NO ONE CAN SNATCH THEM FROM THE FATHER'S HAND."
> —JOHN 10:28–29 (NLT)

In 2011, author and speaker Nancy Guthrie shared about the grief of losing two children to a rare genetic disorder. She wrote, "We trusted God would heal them, and He did. Just not in the way we expected. He took them to be with Him."[2] Her testimony revealed that even in deep sorrow, she found comfort in knowing that her children were held securely in God's hands.

Grief often feels like life has slipped out of control. We may feel helpless, vulnerable, and even abandoned. But Jesus offers a powerful promise: Those who belong to Him are eternally secure in the Father's hands. When loss strikes, this truth is like an anchor in the storm—what is held by God cannot be lost.

Jesus' words remind us that grief doesn't change our standing with Him. We are not forgotten. We are not unprotected. Nothing—not death, pain, or loss—can snatch us out of God's hands. In grief, we cling not only to the memory of our loved ones but to the One who promises eternal life and abiding presence.

This doesn't erase the pain of loss, but it reframes it. It assures us that our life—and the life of those we love—is held within the bigger, eternal story of God. Grief may shift our world, but God's grip never loosens.

Practical Application:

Write down one fear or emotion you've been holding since your loss. Take a few minutes to pray and physically place that note into your Bible as a symbol of releasing it into God's hands.

Reflection:

What helps you feel secure when your emotions are unraveling in grief?

Prayer:

Father, thank You that I am always held in Your hands. When grief makes me feel fragile and fearful, remind me of Your unshakable strength and unending love. Help me to rest in the assurance that I am Yours, forever secure in You. In Jesus' name. Amen.

Read More: Romans 8:38–39; Isaiah 41:10; Psalm 73:23–26; Deuteronomy 33:27; Philippians 1:6

Three

God Is Your Safe Place

"GOD IS OUR REFUGE AND STRENGTH, ALWAYS READY TO HELP IN TIMES OF TROUBLE." —PSALM 46:1 (NLT)

In the days following Hurricane Harvey's devastating impact on Houston in 2017, families were seen clinging to rooftops, waiting to be rescued. One mother, stranded with her children, later shared that though the waters raged around them, she kept whispering Psalm 46:1 aloud: "*God is our refuge and strength.*" She said. "Even when the water rises, He rises higher."[3]

Grief can feel like floodwaters—overwhelming, unrelenting, and impossible to escape. Psalm 46 doesn't deny that troubles come. Instead, it introduces us to a God who meets us in those troubles. He isn't a distant observer; He is our refuge—a shelter we can run into when the emotional storms hit. He is our strength when we have none left. And He is always ready to help.

This verse doesn't offer false hope that pain will vanish overnight. But it assures us that we are never left to face sorrow alone. Our God is not surprised by your heartbreak. He is present in the hospital room, at the graveside, in the silence of long nights, and in the tears that seem to have no end.

Knowing that God is both refuge and strength changes how we grieve. It doesn't eliminate the sorrow, but it anchors our souls in something stronger than pain. God is our steady rock when life feels like it's crumbling beneath us.

Practical Application:

When the ache of loss feels too heavy, take a moment to speak Psalm 46:1 aloud. Let this truth settle into your heart. Write it somewhere visible as a daily reminder: "God is my refuge and strength."

Reflection:

What does it mean to you personally that God is both your refuge and your strength? Where do you need His help most today?

Prayer:

Father, You are my shelter in every storm. When grief shakes me to my core, hold me steady. Remind me that You are close, strong, and always ready to help. Be my strength when I have none of my own. In Jesus' name, Amen.

Read More: Nahum 1:7; Isaiah 41:10; Psalm 91:1–2; 2 Corinthians 12:9–10; Philippians 4:13

Four

God Is Close to the Brokenhearted

"THE LORD IS CLOSE TO THE BROKENHEARTED; HE RESCUES THOSE WHOSE SPIRITS ARE CRUSHED." — PSALM 34:18 (NLT)

After losing her son unexpectedly, Christian author and speaker Kay Warren described grief as a "companion that never leaves." She shared in an interview that in the deepest nights of sorrow, what kept her going was not an explanation but God's presence. "The nearness of God," she said, "was my only lifeline."[4]

Grief has a way of isolating us. It whispers, "No one understands," and tempts us to retreat into silence and despair. Yet the Bible offers a profoundly comforting promise: *"The Lord is close to the brokenhearted."* This is not a generic platitude—it's a deeply personal assurance. God doesn't observe our suffering from afar; He draws near to us in it.

The second part of Psalm 34:18 says God *"rescues those whose spirits are crushed."* The Hebrew phrase implies someone whose strength is gone, whose will is faint. Perhaps you've been there, when just getting out of bed feels impossible, when laughter seems like a distant memory. It is in that fragile space that God draws the nearest. He doesn't wait for us to "get over it." He meets us in the middle of it.

His closeness may not remove the ache instantly, but it sustains us moment by moment. Sometimes, God's nearness shows up through the gentle word of a friend, a song that stirs your soul, or an unexplainable peace that wraps around your heart. His rescue doesn't always look like removal—it often feels like companionship.

Practical Application:

Today, if your heart is heavy, simply whisper, "God, I need You near." Let His nearness become your comfort and His presence be your rescue.

Reflection:

How have you experienced God's closeness in moments of grief or deep sorrow?

Prayer:

Lord, You promise to be near the brokenhearted, and I'm holding onto that promise today. I don't need all the answers—I just need You. Thank You for being close to me, even when I feel crushed. Help me to feel Your presence and know I'm never alone. In Jesus' name. Amen.

Read More: Isaiah 43:2; Matthew 5:4; 2 Corinthians 1:3–4; Psalm 147:3; Romans 8:26–27

Five

When Words Fall Short, God Still Hears

> "The Holy Spirit helps us in our weakness. For example, we don't know what God wants us to pray for. But the Holy Spirit prays for us with groanings that cannot be expressed in words." — Romans 8:26 (NLT)

After losing her infant son, author Nancy Guthrie shared how she often found herself unable to pray. "I would just sit in silence," she wrote, "because I had no words. But over time, I realized that God wasn't waiting for perfect prayers—He was present in my pain, even when I had nothing to say."[5]

Grief has a language of its own—silent sighs, aching stillness, and tear-soaked prayers that never quite reach the lips. Many who walk through sorrow find themselves wordless before God. That can feel unsettling, especially when we've been taught to come before God with eloquent prayers or confident faith.

But Romans 8:26 reminds us that in our weakest moments, when our hearts are too heavy to form coherent words, the Holy Spirit speaks on our behalf. He doesn't need polished prayers; He translates our pain into a language that reaches heaven. This is a profound comfort to the grieving soul: God doesn't require strength from us to hear us. He leans in when all we have is brokenness.

You may not know what to say right now. That's okay. Your silence is not a barrier; it is an invitation for the Holy Spirit to intercede with wordless groans deeper than words. In the rawest moments of grief, your tears and sighs become sacred prayers.

Practical Application:

Don't feel pressured to have the "right" words when praying. Let silence, sighs, or even tears become your offering, knowing the Spirit is translating them into heaven's language.

Reflection:

Have you ever experienced God's comfort when you couldn't find the words to pray?

Prayer:

Holy Spirit, thank You for praying on my behalf when I have no words. My soul feels heavy, and yet You understand what I need even when I don't. Help me trust that You're close, even in the silence. In Jesus' name. Amen.

Read More: Psalm 38:9; Isaiah 40:29; John 14:26; 2 Corinthians 12:9–10; Hebrews 4:15–16

Six

A Song in the Night

> "EACH DAY THE LORD POURS HIS UNFAILING LOVE UPON ME, AND THROUGH EACH NIGHT I SING HIS SONGS, PRAYING TO GOD WHO GIVES ME LIFE." —PSALM 42:8 (NLT)

Horatio Spafford, a 19th-century lawyer, endured immense tragedy. After losing his son to illness and suffering major financial loss, he faced his most painful blow—the death of his four daughters in a shipwreck. While traveling to meet his grieving wife, he penned the hymn "It Is Well with My Soul," testifying to God's peace amid the storm.[6] His grief didn't silence him; it gave birth to a song that has comforted millions.

Grief often steals our words. It leaves us in a place of quiet, aching numbness. Yet in Psalm 42, David reveals a powerful truth: Even in his darkest moments, he sang. Not because the pain was gone, but because God was still with him. His song was a declaration that grief would not have the final say.

Nighttime often intensifies sorrow. The distractions of the day fade, and our thoughts are louder. But David didn't let the night silence his faith. He chose to remember God's love poured out by day and responded with prayer and praise in the night. This rhythm of remembering and responding is crucial in seasons of sorrow.

Like David—and like Spafford—we may not always feel like singing. But our song doesn't have to be perfect. God receives our broken praise. In fact, it's often in the night that He draws closest. Grief doesn't erase worship—it reshapes it. A song in the night is a sign that hope still breathes within.

Practical Application:

Take sometime even in your grief, to listen to God-honoring worship songs. Focus on the lyrics of the music and, if possible, sing along. Feel God's presence pouring out His unfailing love and carrying you through the night.

Reflection Question:

What might your "song in the night" sound like right now—and how could expressing it begin your healing?

Prayer:

God of the day and the night, I invite You into the silence of my sorrow. When I feel empty, remind me of Your love poured out. Teach me to worship and trust You, not because I understand, but because You are faithful. In Jesus' name, Amen.

Read More: Lamentations 3:22–24; Psalm 30:5; Acts 16:25; Isaiah 61:3; 2 Corinthians 4:8–10

Seven

Hope in the Valley of Trouble

"I WILL ... TRANSFORM THE VALLEY OF TROUBLE INTO A GATEWAY OF HOPE." — HOSEA 2:15 (NLT)

After the catastrophic Fire in California, in November 2018, several residents like Steve Crowder lost everything—their homes, businesses, and sense of security. "It's not going to be easy and it's not going to be quick," Crowder said, "but it can be done." Years later, the town rallied to rebuild a beautiful community, one step at a time. [7] What was once a valley of rubble became the gateway of new hope and healing. God turns ruins into renewal.

The Valley of Achor—meaning "Valley of Trouble"—was where Achan's disobedience brought judgment on Israel (Joshua 7). It symbolized guilt, grief, and loss—a reminder of failure and consequence. But in Hosea 2:15, God does something remarkable: He takes that place of pain and renames it a *"gateway of hope."*

Grief often feels like hope is out of reach. Loss whispers that nothing good can come from the valley we're in. But Hosea reminds us that God does His greatest work in our lowest valleys. This shift shows that our past failures, grief, or pain do not limit God. What once marked failure becomes the place of renewal.

The Hebrew word for "*hope*" implies expectation and anticipation—not wishful thinking, but confident trust in God's faithfulness. Just as God restored Israel, He promises to restore us. Our valleys are not our endings—they're often the gateway to new beginnings and unexpected blessings.

Practical Application:

Write down a grief or loss you've experienced and one way God has begun to redeem it—through healing, deeper faith, or relationships. Then pray and ask God to keep turning your *"valley of trouble"* into a *"gateway of hope."*

Reflection:

What is one painful area in your life where you need God to transform trouble into hope?

Prayer:

Lord, I bring You the valleys in my life—those places marked by grief, pain, and confusion. You promise to transform even my deepest troubles into a gateway of hope. Help me to trust that You are working, even when I cannot see it. Bring beauty from ashes and turn my mourning into joy. In Jesus' name, Amen.

Read More: Joshua 7:24–26; Isaiah 61:1–3; Romans 8:28; Psalm 30:5; Joel 2:25

Eight

The Gift of God's Comfort

"GOD BLESSES THOSE WHO MOURN, FOR THEY WILL BE COMFORTED." — MATTHEW 5:4 (NLT)

When Grammy-winning artist Mandisa lost a close friend to suicide, she spiraled into deep depression. But over time, she shared that it was God's Word and presence that slowly brought her out. She said, "Grief doesn't go away, but God's comfort becomes stronger. He meets you right where you are, even in the darkness."[8]

Jesus' words in the Sermon on the Mount may feel paradoxical. How can mourning bring blessing? With God, sorrow is not ignored—it's sacred. Jesus assures us that our grief draws the attention of heaven. To mourn is to open our hearts to God's healing presence.

This beatitude is not a shallow promise of quick relief; it's a deep assurance that God is close to the brokenhearted. His comfort doesn't always erase the pain, but it meets us in the middle of it. Often, His comfort comes through His Word,

His people, His Spirit, and sometimes just through the quiet reminder that we are not alone.

In the moments when grief feels unbearable, we can rest in the truth that Jesus has blessed those who mourn, not because mourning is easy, but because it draws us closer to the Comforter Himself.

Practical Application:

Allow yourself to grieve, knowing that God sees your pain and promises to comfort you. Journal your emotions or talk to someone safe. Invite God's presence into your sorrow.

Reflection:

In what ways have you experienced God's comfort in your season of mourning?

Prayer:

Lord, I bring You my mourning and sorrow. I may not understand this season, but I trust that You bless those who grieve. Let Your comfort surround me like a warm blanket. Meet me in my pain and carry me in Your love. In Jesus' name, Amen.

Read More: Psalm 34:18; Isaiah 61:1–3; John 14:18; 2 Corinthians 1:3–5; Revelation 21:4

Nine

The Hope That Anchors

> "IF OUR HOPE IN CHRIST IS ONLY FOR THIS LIFE, WE ARE MORE TO BE PITIED THAN ANYONE IN THE WORLD." —1 CORINTHIANS 15:19 (NLT)

Holocaust survivor Corrie ten Boom spent months in the Ravensbrück concentration camp during World War II. Despite unimaginable suffering, Corrie clung to her faith in Christ. She wrote, "There is no pit so deep that God's love is not deeper still." Her hope was not rooted in circumstances, but in Christ's promise of eternal life—even when everything around her said otherwise.[9]

Paul's words in 1 Corinthians 15:19 are striking: If Christ has not been raised from the dead, then Christians are to be pitied. Paul is reminding believers that the Christian life isn't just about moral living or temporal blessings. It is centered on the reality of eternity. If resurrection isn't real, then the sacrifices believers make—the suffering endured for the sake of Christ—are meaningless. But **because Jesus rose from the dead, everything changes**.

That means we can endure trials with perseverance, sacrifice with joy, and even face death with peace. The resurrection guarantees that what is currently wrong will be made right, what is broken will be restored, and what is mortal will be given eternal life (1 Corinthians 15:53–54).

This kind of hope acts like an anchor. It stabilizes us in the storms of life and lifts our eyes beyond our struggles. Hope in Christ is confident expectation built on His resurrection. It doesn't eliminate pain, but it gives purpose in pain, knowing that one day, all things will be made new.

Practical Application:

Refuse to let your present pain distort your eternal perspective. Write down one trial you're facing today, and then write a truth from Scripture, perhaps from below, that gives you hope beyond it. Let God's Word anchor your soul.

Reflection:

What would change in your mindset if you truly believed your current suffering was temporary and outweighed by eternal glory?

Prayer:

God of hope, anchor my soul in the truth of the resurrection. Please help me to live with an eternal mindset and to trust that what I suffer now will one day be redeemed. Thank You for the promise of life beyond this world. In Jesus' name, Amen.

Read More: Romans 8:18; 1 Corinthians 2:9; 2 Corinthians 4:16–18; Revelation 21:1–5; 1 Peter 1:3–5

Ten

Worship Through the Tears

> "Job said, 'I came naked from my mother's womb, and I will be naked when I leave. The Lord gave me what I had, and the Lord has taken it away. Praise the name of the Lord!'" —Job 1:21 (NLT)

In 2013, musician TobyMac and his wife, Amanda, lost their 21-year-old son unexpectedly. In the days that followed, TobyMac wrote, "God didn't promise us a life without pain. He promised He would never leave us or forsake us." Despite their unimaginable sorrow, they clung to God's presence through worship, even recording songs born from their grief.[10]

In one day, Job lost all ten of his children and everything he owned. Yet, his first reaction was to worship. He tore his robe, shaved his head—a sign of mourning—but then fell to the ground in reverence to God. Job didn't suppress his pain; he surrendered it.

In grief, we're tempted to withdraw from God or question His goodness. But Job reminds us that worship isn't only for the mountaintop moments—it's for the valleys, too. Job didn't understand the *why*, but he trusted the *One Who Did*.

God's presence does not readily eliminate the pain of grief, but it does help us get through it. Worshipping God in our sorrow brings our hearts back in line with His eternal truth: He is still God, still good, and still with us. And He will eventually restore us, just like He did for Job (Job 42:12–13).

Practical Application:

Write out your honest feelings and prayers about your loss—grief, anger, confusion—and then conclude with one statement of truth about who God is. Let this be your offering to God, like Job did.

Reflection:

How have you seen God's presence sustain you in moments of loss?

Prayer:

Lord, You are still worthy even when my heart is broken. I don't understand all that has happened, but I choose to worship You. Stay near to me. Help me trust You in my sorrow, and give me strength for each new day. In Jesus' name, Amen.

Read More: Psalm 34:18; Isaiah 43:2; John 11:33–35; Lamentations 3:22–24; Romans 8:38–39

Eleven

Never Separated

> "I AM CONVINCED THAT NOTHING CAN EVER SEPARATE US FROM GOD'S LOVE. NEITHER DEATH NOR LIFE, NEITHER ANGELS NOR DEMONS, NEITHER OUR FEARS FOR TODAY NOR OUR WORRIES ABOUT TOMORROW—NOT EVEN THE POWERS OF HELL CAN SEPARATE US FROM GOD'S LOVE." —ROMANS 8:38 (NLT)

After the tragic 2010 Haiti earthquake, many stories of loss and faith emerged. One came from a woman named Marie, who lost her husband and two children beneath the rubble. Despite her grief, she said in an interview, "I still believe in Jesus. My pain is great, but I know He has not left me. His love is the only thing I have left, and it's enough to keep me going."[11]

In the valley of grief, we often feel isolated, like no one understands the depths of our pain. That's where the apostle Paul's words become a lifeline: *"Nothing can separate us from God's love."* Not death. Not fear. Not even the heartbreak that leaves us feeling numb and forgotten.

Paul doesn't offer this as a poetic sentiment but as a powerful, Spirit-breathed truth. When loss shakes everything else loose—our routines, relationships, and sense of control—God's love remains immovable. We might question where God is, but His love never leaves us. In fact, He draws nearer in our sorrow (Psalm 34:18).

God's love is not just a concept—it is a Person (1 John 4:8). Jesus entered into human suffering, wept at the tomb of a friend, and bore the ultimate pain on the cross. That same love now pursues us relentlessly, even in our darkest days.

Practical Application:

Find a quiet space today to sit in God's presence. Read Romans 8:38-39 aloud, replacing the word "us" with your own name. Let the truth settle in your heart: You are never alone in your grief.

Reflection:

How does knowing you are never separated from God's love comfort you in your season of loss?

Prayer:

Father, when I feel abandoned by people or overwhelmed by grief, remind me that nothing can separate me from Your love. Hold me close today. Let Your love be the anchor that keeps me steady in the storm. In Jesus' name, Amen.

Read More: Psalm 23:4; Isaiah 49:15-16; John 14:18; Hebrews 13:5; Psalm 139:7-10

Twelve

You Are Not Alone

> "Do not be afraid or discouraged, for the Lord will personally go ahead of you. He will be with you; he will neither fail you nor abandon you." —Deuteronomy 31:8 (NLT)

In 2017, military widow Michelle Black lost her husband in an ambush in Niger. In the weeks that followed, she was overwhelmed by the weight of grief and the questions that came with it. But she later wrote, "In the darkest season of my life, I discovered that God was already ahead of me, preparing healing in unexpected ways."[12] Her story is a reminder that God's presence does not begin after grief—it walks ahead of us into it.

When Moses addressed the Israelites in Deuteronomy 31, they stood on the edge of an uncertain future. He wouldn't go with them into the Promised Land—but he assured them of something even more important: God would. Not just eventually. Not from a distance. But *"personally."*

Grief is often accompanied by deep loneliness. We may be surrounded by people, yet feel completely alone in our loss. But Scripture promises that the Lord Himself walks beside us every step of the way and goes ahead of us clearing a path for our recovery through the wilderness of sorrow. God doesn't simply send comfort—He is our Comfort (2 Corinthians 1:3-4). He shows up Himself. And when we fear collapsing under the weight of it all, He whispers, *"I will never fail you. I will never abandon you."*

Practical Application:

Every morning this week, begin your day by reading Deuteronomy 31:8. Say it aloud, and ask God to lead you through your grief that day. Remind yourself that you are not entering the unknown alone. God is personally walking beside you and ahead of you.

Reflection:

In what ways have you experienced or longed for God's presence during your grief? What might it mean to trust that He is walking ahead of you?

Prayer:

Lord, I can't always see what's ahead, and the weight of my grief often overwhelms me. But I trust that You are already in my tomorrow. Thank You for going before me and never abandoning me. Give me strength today to follow where You lead. In Jesus' name, Amen.

Read More: Joshua 1:9; Isaiah 43:2; Psalm 34:18; Romans 8:31; John 14:27

Thirteen

The Last Word Belongs to Victory

"But thank God! He gives us victory over sin and death through our Lord Jesus Christ." —1 Corinthians 15:57 (NLT)

In 2020, singer TobyMac lost his 21-year-old son unexpectedly. In the months following, he released a song titled "21 Years,"[13] filled with honest grief and raw questions. But through his music and interviews, he declared his belief in the resurrection: "God didn't promise us a life without pain. He promised He would never leave us. And because of Jesus, I believe we'll see our son again."[14] In the face of loss, TobyMac chose hope—anchored not in feeling but in the risen Christ.

Death feels so final. It steals loved ones, disrupts plans, and reminds us of our human frailty. But Scripture triumphantly declares that we have victory over sin and death—not because of our strength, but through Jesus Christ. The resurrection is God's definitive answer to the brokenness of this world.

This victory is not just about one day rising from the grave; it's about living with confidence today. Christ's resurrection promises that the worst thing is never the last thing. It infuses today's suffering with eternal meaning. *"Death has been swallowed up in victory!"* (1Corinthians 15:54).

When everything in life seems like it's falling apart—when diagnoses are grim, when graves are freshly dug, when tears won't stop—the resurrection whispers, This is not the end. Jesus defeated death, and because He lives, so will we. Hope is not a cliché; it's a resurrected reality.

Practical Application:

Reflect on a loss that still hurts. Now, speak the truth of 1 Corinthians 15:57 aloud over that grief. Write the verse down and place it somewhere visible this week. Let God's victory reframe your sorrow.

Reflection:

How does the resurrection of Jesus shift your perspective on death, grief, and the loss you've experienced?

Prayer:

Risen Lord, thank You that death is not the end. Thank You for the victory You secured through the empty tomb. In my sorrow, help me to live with the hope that because You live, I will live—and so will those who trust in You. In Jesus' name, Amen.

Read More: 1 Corinthians 15:54–55; Romans 8:11; Revelation 21:4; John 11:25–26; 1 Thessalonians 4:13–14

Fourteen

Held in His Hand

"For the life of every living thing is in God's hand, and the breath of every human being." —Job 12:10 (NLT)

In 2018, the world watched as a youth soccer team and their coach were trapped in a flooded cave in Thailand. For 17 days, their lives hung in the balance. When they were miraculously rescued, one of the boys told reporters, "I just kept praying. I believed that God would bring us out."[15] Even in darkness, they clung to the hope that their lives were in God's hands—and He proved faithful.

Job's words in chapter 12 come from a place of deep sorrow. He had lost everything—his wealth, his health, and his children. And yet, in the midst of his grief, Job anchors himself in this truth: Every life, every breath, is held in God's hand.

When grief strikes, it can feel like the world is spinning out of control. We grasp for answers, struggle to breathe under the weight of sorrow, and wonder if we'll ever feel whole again.

But Job reminds us that we are not abandoned. We are held by God's loving hand.

God is not only aware of our pain—He holds us through it. He sees the tears that no one else sees. His hands, which shaped the stars, also cradle our hearts when they break. When the weight of loss threatens to bring us down, the truth that we are still in His hands becomes our lifeline.

Practical Application:

Take a quiet moment today to sit in stillness. Place your hands open in your lap and pray, "God, I rest in Your hands." Visualize your life, your pain, and your grief safely in His care. Let His presence calm your heart.

Reflection:

What would change in your grief if you truly believed that your life—and your loss—are held in God's loving hands?

Prayer:

Father, in the midst of heartache, remind me that You hold me. When life feels fragile, help me find strength in knowing You are near. Thank You that nothing escapes Your notice—not even my quiet tears. Hold me close today. In Jesus' name. Amen.

Read More: Isaiah 41:13; Psalm 139:7–10; John 10:28–29; Deuteronomy 33:27; Romans 8:38–39

Fifteen

No More Tears

"He will wipe every tear from their eyes, and there will be no more death or sorrow or crying or pain. All these things are gone forever."—Revelation 21:4 (NLT)

In 2020, a woman named Ethel, age 95, lost her only son to a sudden illness during the height of the pandemic. In an interview, she said through tears, "I feel the pain every day, but I hold onto the hope that one day I will see him again. God promises a day with no more tears."[16] Her words reflect the longing every grieving heart holds—for a place where sorrow no longer exists.

The book of Revelation closes with a stunning promise: The end of sorrow. John describes a day when God Himself will tenderly wipe away every tear. This is not symbolic language—it's deeply personal. God doesn't just end pain; He addresses it directly. He acknowledges our suffering and promises to remove it forever.

Grief can make us feel like pain will last forever. The days stretch long, the nights even longer. But God assures us that loss is temporary for those in Christ. Death, crying, mourning—all the consequences of a broken world—will one day be erased. Not diminished. Not lessened. Gone.

This hope doesn't ignore our pain—it reframes it. It tells us that our tears have an expiration date. Every aching memory, every goodbye, every painful anniversary will one day be answered with the gentle hand of God. Heaven isn't wishful thinking; it's a secured destination. And the God who made that promise is trustworthy.

Practical Application:

Write Revelation 21:4 on a card or sticky note and place it somewhere you'll see daily. Let it remind you that your grief has an end date, and your hope has a beginning that never ends.

Reflection:

How does knowing that God will personally wipe away every tear give you strength to face today?

Prayer:

Father, I thank You that my pain is not permanent. Thank You for the hope of heaven and the promise that one day, You will wipe away every tear. Until that day, hold me close and help me endure with faith. In Jesus' name, Amen.

Read More: Isaiah 25:8; 1 Thessalonians 4:13–14; Romans 8:18; John 14:1–3; Psalm 30:5

Sixteen

Strength in the Midst of Sorrow

"My soul melts with sorrow; strengthen me according to Your word." —Psalm 119:28 (BSB)

After the unexpected death of her son, author and speaker Kay Warren described days when she could hardly breathe under the weight of grief. In her journal, she wrote, "There is no drug, no distraction, no escape—only the Word of God gives me strength hour by hour."[17] Her words echo the psalmist's cry: when sorrow crushes the soul, God's Word becomes our lifeline.

Grief has a way of draining not only our joy but also our strength. The psalmist's declaration is raw and honest: *"My soul melts with sorrow."* It's a picture of a heart undone—flooded by sadness, depleted of vitality. But he doesn't stop there. He turns his eyes upward and pleads, *"Strengthen me according to Your word."*

God's Word isn't just information—it's fuel for the weary soul. In seasons of loss, Scripture reminds us of God's nearness, His comfort, and His promises. It doesn't eliminate the sorrow, but it infuses strength into the middle of it. The strength God provides doesn't deny pain—it sustains us through it.

When our emotions fail and our spirit feels broken, the Word of God offers eternal truths that do not change: *"The Lord is close to the brokenhearted"* (Psalm 34:18), *"Weeping may last through the night, but joy comes with the morning"* (Psalm 30:5), and *"Nothing can separate us from God's love"* (Romans 8:39). These promises don't make grief disappear, but they anchor us so we don't sink in it.

Practical Application:

Choose one Bible verse that speaks directly to your current pain and write it down. Memorize it, meditate on it, and repeat it in moments of sorrow. Let God's Word be your strength when everything else feels weak.

Reflection:

What Scripture has helped you find strength in your most sorrowful moments?

Prayer:

God, my soul is weary from grief. Some days I feel like I can't go on. But I choose to lean on Your Word for strength. Speak life and hope into my heart through Your promises. Anchor me in Your truth, and carry me through the sorrow. In Jesus' name, Amen.

Read More: Isaiah 40:29; Psalm 46:1; 2 Corinthians 1:3–4; Psalm 34:17–18; Joshua 1:9

Seventeen

Peace in the Middle of Pain

"I HAVE TOLD YOU ALL THIS SO THAT YOU MAY HAVE PEACE IN ME. HERE ON EARTH, YOU WILL HAVE MANY TRIALS AND SORROWS. BUT TAKE HEART, BECAUSE I HAVE OVERCOME THE WORLD."
—JOHN 16:33 (NLT)

In 2015, when missionary doctor Kent Brantly contracted Ebola while serving in Liberia. Facing the very real possibility of death, he later recalled in an interview, "Even when I was sure I was going to die, I had an inexplicable peace. I was not afraid, because I knew Christ had already won."[18] His calm amid crisis reflected a deeper truth: the peace Jesus offers doesn't depend on circumstances.

Jesus never promised a life free from grief, pain, or loss. In fact, He clearly said, *"Here on earth you will have many trials and sorrows."* That's the reality of life in a broken world. But the power of His words lies in the next phrase: *"Take heart, because I have overcome the world."*

In moments of intense grief—when the hospital calls, when the casket closes, when the silence at home is deafening—it's easy to believe the pain will consume us. But Jesus says we can have peace in Him. Not in the absence of trouble, but in the presence of our Overcomer.

Christ's victory over sin, suffering, and death doesn't mean we escape sorrow—it means our sorrow doesn't have the final say. Through Christ, we are more than victims of loss. We are embraced by the One who conquered the grave, and we are offered peace that cannot be shaken by this world's pain.

Practical Application:

Take five minutes today to sit in silence and reflect on Jesus' promise of peace. Invite Him into your grief. Even if you don't feel peace yet, confess your trust that He has overcome the pain you're facing.

Reflection:

How does Jesus' victory give you hope even when your world feels shattered?

Prayer:

Jesus, You know what it means to suffer, and You never promised I wouldn't. But You did promise peace in You, even in pain. Help me to take heart and believe that You have overcome everything that weighs me down. Be my peace today. In Jesus' name, Amen.

Read More: Romans 5:1; Philippians 4:6–7; Psalm 29:11; 2 Thessalonians 3:16; Isaiah 26:3

Eighteen

Through the Waters and Flames

"When you go through deep waters, I will be with you. When you go through rivers of difficulty, you will not drown. When you walk through the fire of oppression, you will not be burned up; the flames will not consume you." —Isaiah 43:2 (NLT)

In 2013, the Yarnell Hill Fire tragically took the lives of 19 firefighters in Arizona. One survivor, Brendan McDonough, shared that during the chaos, what sustained him wasn't his strength, but the overwhelming sense that God was with him. He later dedicated his life to helping others find hope and healing through their trauma.[19] In moments of fear and grief, the presence of God was his anchor.

Grief often feels like being swept away by a flood or consumed by fire. The chaos is overwhelming, the pain intense, and the journey unrelenting. But Isaiah 43:2 reminds us that God doesn't promise to remove the waters or extinguish the flames. He promises to go with us through them.

This verse speaks to the heart of what it means to suffer with faith. God doesn't avoid our pain—He steps into it. He is present in hospital rooms, beside fresh graves, and in the silence of lonely nights. His promise isn't that we won't feel pain, but that pain will not destroy us. Our grief may leave scars, but not ruin.

The waters will rise, and the fires may rage—but God says, *"You will not drown. You will not be consumed."* His presence doesn't always change our circumstances, but it always changes us in the midst of them.

Practical Application:

Write down one area of your grief or loss that feels overwhelming right now. Then next to it, write Isaiah 43:2. Let God's promise of presence and protection speak louder than the sorrow you carry.

Reflection:

What does it mean to you that God is with you in your suffering, not just watching from a distance?

Prayer:

God, when the waters of sorrow rise and the fire of loss burns hot, remind me that You are near. Please help me to believe that I am not alone and will not be destroyed. Walk with me through this season, and carry me when I cannot walk. In Jesus' name, Amen.

Read More: Psalm 23:4; Matthew 28:20; 2 Corinthians 4:8–9; Deuteronomy 31:6; Romans 8:35–39

Nineteen

Waiting with Hope

> "IF MORTALS DIE, CAN THEY LIVE AGAIN? THIS THOUGHT GIVES ME HOPE, SO I KEEP ON LOOKING FOR THE DAY OF MY RELEASE."
> —JOB 14:14 (NLT)

In 2020, actor Nick Cordero battled COVID-19 for over 90 days before tragically passing. Throughout his hospitalization, his wife Amanda Kloots kept posting updates, encouraging others to hope and pray—even when the outcome was uncertain. She later said, "Hope kept me going. Even when the answers didn't come, the hope still mattered."[20] In the midst of unknowns, hope gives us permission to wait with purpose.

Job asked a question humanity has pondered for millennia: *"If mortals die, can they live again?"* But he didn't stop at uncertainty—he chose to hope. In a time of unimaginable loss and suffering, Job looked beyond his present pain and fixed his eyes on something eternal. That's what grief demands of us—not that we ignore our sorrow, but that we hold tightly to the possibility of restoration.

This verse is powerful because it recognizes the weight of death while clinging to a God who holds life beyond it. Job's suffering was real. His wounds were deep. Yet his spirit whispered, "This isn't the end." Hope gave him reason to wait, to breathe, to carry on.

In grief, time feels frozen, and release seems far away. But like Job, we can choose to hope—not because we deny our pain, but because we believe God's promises are stronger than the grave. Our waiting is not in vain. God is at work even in the silence, preparing a day when tears will be wiped away and mourning will be no more.

Practical Application:

Today, choose one area of grief where you're still waiting for healing or clarity. Write a short prayer of hope, affirming your belief that God is not finished yet—even in what feels final.

Reflection:

How can Job's honest hope in the middle of suffering inspire your own faith as you wait on God?

Prayer:

God, I confess that I don't always understand Your timing or Your ways. But like Job, I choose to hope. Even in the pain, even in the waiting, I trust that You hold life beyond my loss. Please help me to wait with faith, believing that release will come. In Jesus' name, Amen.

Read More: Romans 8:24–25; Lamentations 3:21–23; John 11:25–26; Isaiah 40:31; Revelation 21:4

Twenty

Death Is Not the End

> "Then, when our dying bodies have been transformed into bodies that will never die, this Scripture will be fulfilled: 'Death is swallowed up in victory.'" —1 Corinthians 15:54 (NLT)

In 2019, when author and speaker Rachel Held Evans died unexpectedly at the age of 37, the Christian community mourned deeply. At her memorial, a speaker said, "Rachel is not gone—she is home." That simple phrase reminded everyone present that death, for the believer, is not an ending—it's a homecoming.[21]

Paul's declaration in 1 Corinthians 15:54 is one of the most hope-filled promises in all of Scripture. Though death seems powerful, the resurrection of Jesus changes the narrative. Paul reminds us that there is a day coming when our frail, mortal bodies will be transformed—when death itself will be defeated forever.

Grief whispers that death wins. It shows us tombstones, empty chairs, and tear-stained pillows. But Scripture shouts louder: *"Death is swallowed up in victory!"* The resurrection of Jesus ensures that every believer will one day rise. When you stand beside a casket or walk through the fog of loss, let this verse anchor your soul. It doesn't pretend that loss doesn't hurt—it only guarantees that it won't last. Our dying bodies will be changed. Our tears will be wiped away. Our separation will be swallowed by reunion. In Christ, we grieve with hope, because the cross defeated death and the resurrection opened eternity.

Practical Application:

Reflect on a personal loss and declare aloud this truth: "Death is swallowed up in victory." Let the words become your anchor as you speak life over your sorrow.

Reflection Question:

How does believing in the resurrection shift the way you view the pain of death and loss?

Prayer:

Lord, thank You for the promise that death is not the end. Even in my grief, help me to cling to the truth that You have swallowed death in victory. Let that truth give me hope when my heart aches. Remind me that what feels final now is only the beginning of forever with You. In Jesus' name, Amen.

Read More: John 11:25–26; Philippians 3:20–21; Revelation 21:4; Romans 6:5; 2 Timothy 1:10

Twenty-One

You Are Not Alone

> "Even when I walk through the darkest valley, I will not be afraid, for you are close beside me. Your rod and your staff protect and comfort me." —Psalm 23:4 (NLT)

After losing her son unexpectedly, author and counselor Kay Warren shared in an interview how the silence of grief overwhelmed her. But she also described a quiet comforts she could not explain—what she later called the "presence that holds." "God didn't always say much," she said, "but I never felt alone."[22] Even in her deepest sorrow, God's nearness became her anchor.

Psalm 23:4 is one of the most comforting promises in Scripture. It doesn't deny the existence of *"the darkest valley"*—it acknowledges it boldly. Grief can feel like that: a shadowed, unfamiliar terrain where light seems far away. But David writes not just about the valley, but about the Shepherd who walks with us in it.

In seasons of deep sorrow, we may not hear thunderous answers or feel immediate healing. But Scripture assures us of something even more important—God's presence. His *"rod and staff"* are not abstract symbols; they are tools of guidance, protection, and gentle correction. He does not watch us suffer from a distance. He walks beside us.

You may not be able to explain the ache or understand why this loss occurred. But you don't walk this road alone. The Shepherd of your soul is near, steadying your steps, wiping your tears, and whispering, "I am with you."

Practical Application:

Pause today to invite God into your grief, even if you don't feel Him. Say aloud, "You are with me." Let that truth sink in, especially in your loneliest moments.

Reflection:

When have you most sensed God's nearness during a difficult season? How does knowing He is with you bring comfort today?

Prayer:

Lord, thank You for walking with me through the darkest valleys. I confess that grief can feel lonely, but Your Word reminds me that I am never alone. Be near to me, protect me, and comfort me with Your steady presence. In Jesus' name, Amen.

Read More: Isaiah 43:2; Hebrews 13:5; Psalm 34:18; Deuteronomy 31:8; Romans 8:38–39

Twenty-Two

Life Beyond the Grave

> "JESUS TOLD HER, 'I AM THE RESURRECTION AND THE LIFE.
> ANYONE WHO BELIEVES IN ME WILL LIVE, EVEN AFTER DYING.'"
> —JOHN 11:25 (NLT)

After losing his 10-year-old daughter to a sudden illness, musician Steven Curtis Chapman struggled with unimaginable sorrow. But he found deep comfort in Jesus' words from John 11. At her memorial, he said, "This is not the end of her story. Because of Jesus, we'll see her again."[23] That conviction—that death isn't the final word—became an anchor in his journey through grief.

In John 11, Jesus arrives after His friend Lazarus has died. Martha meets Him, crushed with sorrow and filled with questions. It's in that moment of grief that Jesus declares one of the most powerful promises in Scripture: *"I am the resurrection and the life."* He doesn't just offer resurrection—He is resurrection. His presence brings hope where there seems to be none.

Jesus didn't minimize Martha's pain. He didn't offer shallow platitudes. Instead, He gave her a person—Himself. And that makes all the difference in our grief as well. We're not just holding onto vague comfort. We're clinging to a living Savior who conquered death and offers eternal life to all who believe.

Grief is real, but so is resurrection. Because of Christ, the grave is not the end—it's the doorway to life everlasting. Our loved ones who died in the Lord are not lost; they are alive in Him. And we will see them again.

Practical Application:

Take time today to write the name of a loved one you've lost. Beneath it, write the words Jesus spoke: "I am the resurrection and the life." Let His promise reshape your grief with hope.

Reflection:

How does Jesus' promise in John 11:25 bring comfort to you as you think about the person or people you've lost?

Prayer:

Resurrected Savior, thank You for being the source of eternal life. When I'm overwhelmed by grief, remind me that You hold victory over death. Help me to live with hope and peace, knowing that this life is not the end. In Jesus' name. Amen.

Read More: 1 Thessalonians 4:13–14; Revelation 1:17–18; Romans 6:4–5; 2 Corinthians 5:1; John 14:1–3

Twenty-Three

Christ Defeated Death

> "Now Christ Jesus has come to offer us God's gift of undeserved grace. Christ our Savior defeated death and brought us the good news. It shines like a light and offers life that never ends." —2 Timothy 1:10 (CEV)

Reflecting on the death of his younger brother, Billy, author and pastor Tim Keller said, "The only way to face suffering and death is to face them knowing that Jesus went through them first—and that He conquered them."[24] For Keller, the gospel wasn't just theological—it was personal. Christ's victory over death became his hope in the darkness of loss.

Grief has a way of dimming everything around us. The days feel longer, joy feel distant, and the weight of absence feel unbearable. But Paul reminds us that the gospel shines like a light even in our darkest moments. Jesus has defeated death in real, life-altering power. That victory means our grief is not permanent, and our sorrow does not get the final say.

Christ's resurrection offers more than a future promise; it gives us present peace. Death is the broken gate that Jesus shattered through to bring us into eternal life. The gift of *"undeserved grace"* Paul speaks of isn't earned; it's freely given. And that gift includes the assurance that we will live with Him forever, reunited with those we've lost in Christ.

The good news of the gospel is not that grief disappears—it's that grace shines brighter. Jesus' triumph over death breaks the power of despair and gives us courage to live, love, and hope again.

Practical Application:

When grief feels overwhelming, speak out loud today's verse: "Christ our Savior defeated death." Declare it over your heart, your memories, and your fears. Let His truth become your anchor.

Reflection:

What does it mean to you personally that Jesus defeated death? How does this shape the way you grieve?

Prayer:

Jesus, thank You for defeating death and shining light into my darkest places. When I am burdened by grief, remind me that You've already won. Help me to walk through loss with the unshakable hope that life with You never ends. In Jesus' name, Amen.

Read More: Hebrews 2:14–15; John 11:25–26; Romans 8:38–39; Revelation 21:4; Psalm 27:13–14

Twenty-Four

Rest for the Weary Heart

> "Jesus said, 'Come to me, all of you who are weary and carry heavy burdens, and I will give you rest. Take my yoke upon you. Let me teach you, because I am humble and gentle at heart, and you will find rest for your souls.'" — Matthew 11:28–29 (NLT)

After the loss of his son, songwriter Chris Quilala of Jesus Culture band shared how he struggled with heartbreak and questions, yet in that deep sorrow, he said he felt God's nearness like never before. "I didn't have the answers, but I had His presence," Quilala reflected. "And that was enough to bring peace."[25]

Grief is heavy. It drains strength, clouds the mind, and weighs on the soul. Jesus does not ignore that weight—He speaks directly to it. In Matthew 11, He invites all who are weary and burdened to come to Him. This is not a command to be stronger but an invitation to collapse into His arms.

Jesus offers a different kind of rest. He offers soul-rest. In our grieving, Jesus becomes both Teacher and Companion. He doesn't rush us past the pain but walks gently with us through it. His humility and gentleness assure us that we don't have to pretend to be okay. We can come as we are—confused, broken, angry, numb—and still be received and restored.

This kind of rest doesn't mean the absence of pain, but the presence of peace in the middle of it. The *"yoke"* Jesus speaks of isn't another burden—it's a shared walk, where He does the heavy lifting and teaches us how to breathe again, hope again, and live again.

Practical Application:

Take five minutes today to sit silently before God. As you breathe in, whisper, "Come to me..." As you breathe out, whisper, "And I will give you rest." Let His presence quiet your soul.

Reflection:

What burden are you carrying today that Jesus is inviting you to release into His hands?

Prayer:

Lord Jesus, I bring You the heavy grief I've been carrying. Teach me how to rest in You. Help me to stop striving and instead lean into Your gentle love. Thank You for carrying me through what feels too heavy to bear. In Jesus' name, Amen.

Read More: Psalm 23:1–3; Isaiah 40:29–31; John 14:27; 2 Corinthians 1:3–4; Philippians 4:6–7

Twenty-Five

Joy Will Come Again

> "...His favor lasts a lifetime! Weeping may last through the night, but joy comes with the morning." — Psalm 30:5 (NLT)

After tragically losing her son, author Kay Warren shared about the long nights of weeping and overwhelming sorrow she endured. Yet through tears, she also testified to the flickers of joy that slowly returned, not erasing the pain but gently renewing her soul. "Grief and joy can coexist," she said. "We live in the tension of sorrow and hope."[26]

Grief is like a long, dark night. The hours feel endless, the silence is deafening, and everything familiar seems shadowed by loss. But Scripture promises this: the night will not last forever. God assures us that joy—real, soul-healing joy—will come with the morning.

Psalm 30:5 is not a denial of sorrow but a declaration of God's enduring presence through it. Our tears are real. Our nights are long. But our hope is longer. God's favor isn't short-lived or conditional—it is everlasting. Even when life unravels, His love and goodness remain constant, like a sunrise on the horizon.

This verse doesn't minimize your grief; it anchors it in a bigger promise. You may not know when the "morning" will come, but you can be confident it will. In God's hands, the weeping of now gives way to the wonder of what's ahead. Resurrection joy is coming—not just one day in eternity, but glimpses even now.

Practical Application:

Light a candle as a symbol of hope. As it flickers, thank God that no night lasts forever. Pray for renewed joy to begin rising in your heart, even if only a spark today.

Reflection:

In what area of your life do you need to be reminded that joy will come again?

Prayer:

Father, I am in a season of weeping, and the night feels so long. Remind me that Your joy is not lost—it is simply waiting for the right morning. Let Your favor sustain me, and help me believe again that laughter and light will return. In Jesus' name, Amen.

Read More: Lamentations 3:22–23; John 16:20; Isaiah 61:1–3; Romans 15:13; Revelation 21:4

Twenty-Six

When Life Knocks You Down

"THE LORD UPHOLDS ALL WHO FALL AND LIFTS UP ALL WHO ARE BOWED DOWN." — PSALM 145:14 (NIV)

Rick and Kay Warren, co-founders of Saddleback Church, were open about their grief journey when their son committed suicide following a lifetime fight with mental illness. In one of her reflections, Kay wrote, "I discovered that God doesn't always lift the load, but He always lifts me."[27] Their story is a testament to how the Lord gently lifts up the brokenhearted—even when the pain feels unbearable.

Grief often feels like being knocked to the ground, crushed under the weight of loss and sorrow. It's not just emotional—it's physical, spiritual, and relational. You may feel bowed down by pain, regret, or overwhelming sadness. Psalm 145:14 is a quiet but powerful reminder that God sees you right where you've fallen—and He doesn't leave you there.

The same God who upholds galaxies (Hebrews 1:3, ESV) also upholds the grieving. He reaches down into our lowest moments, not with condemnation, but with compassion. He doesn't ask us to rise on our own. He lifts. He sustains. He restores. And even when you feel too weak to pray, too numb to hope, or too tired to stand—He is present. His *"upholding"* isn't just spiritual encouragement; it's divine intervention. God's character is unchanging, and His tenderness toward the crushed is one of His most beautiful attributes.

Practical Application:

Take a few minutes to sit in stillness. Imagine Jesus kneeling beside you, lifting your chin, reminding you that He's not only with you but holding you up. Ask Him to carry you through this day with His strength.

Reflection:

Where in your life do you feel like you've been knocked down—and how might God be inviting you to let Him lift you?

Prayer:

Lord, I feel overwhelmed, weary, and bowed down by sorrow. I can't carry this alone. Thank You that You don't expect me to. Lift me, hold me, and walk with me through this valley. I trust that Your arms are underneath me, steady and strong. In Jesus' name, Amen.

Read More: Isaiah 40:29–31; Matthew 11:28–30; Psalm 34:18; 2 Corinthians 1:3–4; Isaiah 46:4

Twenty-Seven

Understanding Will Come Later

"JESUS REPLIED, 'YOU DON'T UNDERSTAND NOW WHAT I AM DOING, BUT SOMEDAY YOU WILL.'" —JOHN 13:7 (NLT)

After losing her husband in a car accident, author and speaker Lisa Harper struggled with the unanswered "why." Years later, while speaking to others about grief and redemption, she wrote, "I wouldn't have chosen this pain, but I've seen how God uses broken pieces to build something sacred."[28] Her story echoes the truth Jesus shared with His disciples—that there are times we won't understand what He's doing until much later.

When Jesus spoke these words in John 13, He was washing His disciples' feet—an act of humility and service they couldn't fully grasp. But He knew that greater confusion was coming. In the hours ahead, He would be arrested, crucified, and buried. To them, it would feel like the end of hope. Yet Jesus reassured them that understanding would come later.

This verse speaks tenderly to those who grieve. In our moments of loss, we ask, "Why, God?" But often, heaven is silent—not because God doesn't care, but because the story isn't finished. Some answers are reserved for eternity. Others unfold gradually, as healing comes and purpose begins to surface in the aftermath of pain.

Jesus never asked His followers to understand everything. He simply asked them to trust Him. His perspective is eternal. He sees the tapestry while we only see the tangled threads. Trusting God doesn't eliminate sorrow, but it anchors us through it, with the promise that clarity will come.

Practical Application:

When you're tempted to demand answers from God, shift your focus to trusting His heart. Write down one area of grief where you still don't understand, and surrender it to Him with the words, "I trust You anyway."

Reflection:

What loss or pain in your life do you still struggle to understand—and how might Jesus be inviting you to trust Him in the mystery?

Prayer:

Jesus, there's so much I don't understand. My heart aches with questions. But I believe You see the whole picture and that one day I will understand. Until then, help me trust Your heart, even in the dark. In Jesus' name, Amen.

Read More: Proverbs 3:5–6; Romans 8:28; Isaiah 55:8–9; Ecclesiastes 3:11; 1 Corinthians 13:12

Twenty-Eight

Still Standing

> "WE ARE PRESSED ON EVERY SIDE BY TROUBLES, BUT WE ARE NOT CRUSHED. WE ARE PERPLEXED, BUT NOT DRIVEN TO DESPAIR. WE ARE HUNTED DOWN, BUT NEVER ABANDONED BY GOD. WE GET KNOCKED DOWN, BUT WE ARE NOT DESTROYED. THROUGH SUFFERING, OUR BODIES CONTINUE TO SHARE IN THE DEATH OF JESUS SO THAT THE LIFE OF JESUS MAY ALSO BE SEEN IN OUR BODIES." — 2 CORINTHIANS 4:8–10 (NLT)

In 2010, a massive earthquake devastated Haiti, claiming over 200,000 lives. In the rubble of Port-au-Prince, a group of Christians gathered under a tarp and began singing. A journalist reported hearing them declare in unison, "We are still here. We are still standing."[29] Even in the face of unimaginable loss, they proclaimed hope. Their faith echoed Paul's words to the Corinthians.

Paul doesn't sugarcoat suffering. He acknowledges it. But he also proclaims a deeper truth—none of it ends in destruction. Though grief presses in, it doesn't crush us. Though sorrow clouds our minds, it doesn't steal our hope. Why? Because God's sustaining presence holds us together.

This passage reminds us that the presence of pain does not mean the absence of God. God is often most present in our lowest moments. Our suffering does not cancel God's promises. Instead, it creates space for His strength to be revealed. Like cracked vessels holding light, our brokenness allows the glory of God to shine through. Even when we're knocked down, we're not destroyed—because God is with us.

Practical Application:

List the ways grief has pressed or knocked you down. Then, beside each one, write how God has helped you endure even in the pain. Let it become a record of His sustaining grace.

Reflection:

Which phrase from 2 Corinthians 4:8–10 speaks most deeply to your current experience, and why?

Prayer:

Father, when I feel pressed, confused, or weary, remind me that I am not alone. You are sustaining me even when I don't feel strong. Let my life be a testimony that though I may be broken, I am never forsaken. Shine through my scars. In Jesus' name, Amen.

Read More: Isaiah 43:2; Psalm 34:19; Romans 5:3–5; 2 Corinthians 1:3–5; Philippians 4:13

Twenty-Nine

Their Work Will Follow Them

"I HEARD A VOICE FROM HEAVEN SAYING, 'BLESSED ARE THOSE WHO DIE IN THE LORD FROM NOW ON. YES,' SAYS THE SPIRIT, 'THEY ARE BLESSED INDEED, FOR THEY WILL REST FROM THEIR HARD WORK; FOR THEIR GOOD DEEDS FOLLOW THEM!'" — REVELATION 14:13 (NLT)

Dr. Paul Brand was a missionary surgeon who pioneered reconstructive techniques for leprosy patients in India. After his death, many of his patients, colleagues, and students described how his quiet faith and compassion changed their lives. His legacy didn't die with him—it lived on in others.[30]

Grief often brings the aching fear that everything our loved ones stood for, gave, and built have vanished with them. But Scripture paints a more comforting picture. In Revelation 14:13, God assures us that those who *"die in the Lord"* are not only blessed, but their deeds endure, long after their final breath.

Their work—whether public or unseen, simple or significant—is not forgotten. The acts of love, prayers, sacrifices, and kindness they showed continue to make a lasting impact in the world. The *"good deeds"* of those we've lost are remembered by God and passed on through the lives they touched.

This gives tremendous hope. The legacy of those who've gone before us is not erased. Their influence still inspires, teaches, and comforts. And one day, we too will join that great cloud of witnesses—resting in Christ and knowing our lives mattered because they were anchored in Him.

Practical Application:

Think of someone you've lost who lived a life of faith. What is one thing they did that still influences you today. How can you honor their legacy in the way you live?

Reflection:

How does knowing that "their good deeds follow them" shift your view of death and legacy?

Prayer:

Lord, thank You for the lives of those who walked in faith before me. Their work, their love, their sacrifices weren't wasted—they live on in me and others. Please help me to live in such a way that my deeds will also follow me in faithfulness. In Jesus' name, Amen.

Read More: 1 Corinthians 15:58; Hebrews 6:10; Philippians 1:21; 2 Timothy 4:7–8; John 12:24–26

Thirty

Comforted to Comfort Others

> "HE COMFORTS US IN ALL OUR TROUBLES SO THAT WE CAN COMFORT OTHERS. WHEN THEY ARE TROUBLED, WE WILL BE ABLE TO GIVE THEM THE SAME COMFORT GOD HAS GIVEN US." — 2 CORINTHIANS 1:4 (NLT)

After losing her teenage son, Kay Warren, co-founder of Saddleback Church, discovered a renewed purpose: helping others navigate their loss. Her vulnerability became a lifeline to grieving families who didn't know where to turn.[31] Her story reminds us that comfort received becomes comfort shared.

Grief can feel isolating, overwhelming, and endless. Amid deep sorrow, Paul reminds us of a divine reality: God comforts us not just to ease our pain, but to equip us to comfort others. God's healing touch is not a dead end—it's a channel. When we experience the peace of His presence in the midst of grief, it becomes a resource we can pass on to others who are suffering.

This doesn't mean you must have all the answers or that you must be fully healed before helping others. Sometimes, simply sitting in silence with someone, offering a shared tear, or saying "I understand" can carry more comfort than a thousand words. God uses our wounds to heal others. He repurposes our pain into ministry.

Grief will always hurt, but it doesn't have to be wasted. When you allow God's comfort to flow through you to someone else, your story becomes part of their healing. In that way, even in loss, love continues to give.

Practical Application:

Reach out to someone you know who is grieving. Offer to pray for them, or simply listen without trying to fix anything. Let your own journey of grief become a bridge of hope for someone else.

Reflection:

How has God comforted you in your grief, and who might need that same comfort today?

Prayer:

Father, thank You for not abandoning me in my sorrow. Your comfort has sustained me when I felt broken. Help me be a channel of that same comfort to someone else in need today. Let my pain not be wasted, but transformed into healing for others. In Jesus' name, Amen.

Read More: Isaiah 66:13; Psalm 147:3; Romans 12:15; Galatians 6:2; Matthew 5:4

Thirty-One

Because He Lives

> "Christ has indeed been raised from the dead, the firstfruits of those who have fallen asleep." —1 Corinthians 15:20 (NIV)

On Easter Sunday 2020, in the midst of the COVID-19 pandemic, the Brooklyn Tabernacle streamed a worship service to an empty sanctuary. As the choir sang "Because He Lives," hope echoed through a fearful, grieving world. Pastor Jim Cymbala later shared that messages poured in from around the globe—people found peace and renewed strength in the reminder that Jesus had conquered the grave.[32]

Paul declares in 1 Corinthians 15:20, "Christ has indeed been raised from the dead." This isn't speculation—it's certainty. Calling Jesus the "firstfruits" means His resurrection is the promise and preview of ours. In Scripture, the firstfruits of a harvest were an offering that guaranteed more to come.

Because Christ rose, death is no longer the end but a passage into God's presence. Resurrection is not wishful thinking—it's a historical reality with eternal impact. We still grieve, but not as those without hope (1 Thessalonians 4:13). The empty tomb means separation is temporary, reunion is certain, and the best is still ahead.

Practical Application:

Take a moment today to write a letter to someone you've lost—express your grief honestly, but also declare the hope you have because of Christ's resurrection. Let it be a spiritual exercise that turns sorrow into praise.

Reflection:

How does knowing that Christ's resurrection guarantees your own resurrection bring peace to your current grief?

Prayer:

Risen Savior, thank You for conquering death and giving me hope that extends beyond the grave. When I face sorrow and separation, remind me that You are alive and preparing a place for me. Help me live today in light of eternity. In Jesus' name, Amen.

Read More: John 11:25–26; 1 Thessalonians 4:13–14; Romans 6:4–5; Revelation 1:17–18; 2 Corinthians 4:14

Thirty-Two

A Promise You Can Count On

> "Don't let your hearts be troubled. Trust in God, and trust also in me. There is more than enough room in my Father's home. If this were not so, would I have told you that I am going to prepare a place for you?" —John 14:1–2 (NLT)

When Randy Alcorn's daughter was little, he told her that heaven is a real place prepared by Jesus for those who believe. Years later, after his mother's death, those same words comforted him: "Heaven isn't a vague dream—it's our real home, more real than anything on earth."[33] In times of grief, the reality of heaven becomes more than theology—it becomes hope.

Grief can shake us. It can make the world feel uncertain, even terrifying. When Jesus spoke the words in John 14, He was preparing His disciples for His impending death. He knew they would be afraid, confused, and heartbroken. So He gave them a gift before His suffering—a promise of heaven.

Jesus doesn't offer empty comfort. He invites us to trust Him. Not just believe in Him, but to entrust our hearts to Him. Why? Because He's already made arrangements for us. Heaven is not some distant hope—it is a home prepared by Christ Himself for His people. And that truth provides deep assurance for every believer navigating grief.

This promise means that loss is not the end. For those who have trusted in Christ, death is not a closed door—it's a passage to the home Jesus has prepared. This gives us a future hope that reshapes our present sorrow. It gives us permission to grieve with peace, knowing the story isn't over.

Practical Application:

Take a few moments today to write a note to someone you've lost—share with them the hope you now cling to because of Jesus' promise. Let it be a spiritual release and a declaration of faith.

Reflection:

How does Jesus' promise of preparing a place for you in heaven bring comfort in your season of loss?

Prayer:

Lord Jesus, thank You for going before me and preparing a place I can call home with You. When grief weighs down my heart, remind me that Your promise is sure and eternal. Help me trust You even when life feels uncertain. In Jesus' name. Amen.

Read More: Revelation 21:4; Philippians 3:20–21; 2 Corinthians 5:1; Psalm 23:6; Hebrews 13:14

Thirty-Three

A Reunion is Coming

> "IF I GO AND PREPARE A PLACE FOR YOU, I WILL COME BACK AND TAKE YOU TO BE WITH ME THAT YOU ALSO MAY BE WHERE I AM. YOU KNOW THE WAY TO THE PLACE WHERE I AM GOING."
> —JOHN 14:3–4 (NIV)

When missionary Amy Carmichael was ministering in India, she often comforted orphans who had lost their families by telling them about heaven—not as a distant dream, but as a promised reunion. [34] In a time when grief was overwhelming, this hope of being reunited brought comfort to her and countless others.

These verses are among the most comforting in Scripture. Before His crucifixion, Jesus promised His disciples, "I will come back and take you to be with me." It was a pledge of eternal fellowship, not just salvation.

Grief can make us feel distant from God, but Jesus' words cut through that pain: "You are not forgotten—I'm coming for you." Heaven isn't only a place; it's being with Him. Every tear shed at a graveside will one day be answered with reunion with our loved ones and with Jesus, face to face.

We can live with confidence, knowing the pain of parting is temporary and that Christ Himself will bring us safely home.

Practical Application:

Spend time meditating on the hope of heaven, not as an abstract idea but as a reunion with Christ. Consider writing out a note thanking God for the loved ones you'll one day see again in His presence.

Reflection:

How does Jesus' promise of personally returning for you affect your perspective on grief and eternity?

Prayer:

Lord, thank You that You are preparing a place for me and that You will return to bring me home. In moments of loss and loneliness, help me cling to Your promise of eternal reunion. Let that hope sustain me today. In Jesus' name, Amen.

Read More: 1 Thessalonians 4:13–18; Revelation 22:12; Titus 2:13; Isaiah 25:8; Philippians 1:23

Thirty-Four

We Belong to the Lord

> "If we live, it's to honor the Lord. And if we die, it's to honor the Lord. So whether we live or die, we belong to the Lord." —Romans 14:8 (NLT)

When missionary Elisabeth Elliot lost her husband, Jim Elliot, who was killed by the very people he tried to reach, her grief was deep. Yet she wrote, "The deepest things I've learned have come from the deepest suffering." She lived the rest of her life anchored in one truth—whether in life or death, we belong to God.[35]

Paul's words in Romans 14:8 offer one of the most comforting truths for those walking through grief: we belong to the Lord. This isn't a conditional belonging—it's a permanent identity, whether we're in the prime of life or at death's door. There is no moment, not even the sting of death, when we are outside His loving possession.

For the grieving, this truth lifts a heavy burden. It assures us that the ones we've lost in Christ are not lost to Him. They are still His. And we, too, are securely held in His hands. Our lives have purpose as long as we breathe, and even our death honors Him because it ushers us into eternal communion with Him.

This verse reminds us that death does not define us—our belonging to Christ does. Grief becomes a journey not just of mourning, but of remembering who we are and whose we are.

Practical Application:

Take a moment today to say out loud: "I belong to the Lord." Let those words become a declaration over your grief and a reassurance of His unchanging love for you and for those who have passed in Christ.

Reflection:

How does knowing that you and your loved one belong to the Lord change the way you experience grief?

Prayer:

Lord, thank You that whether in life or death, I am Yours. Help me to rest in the truth that I am never outside of Your care. Remind me that those I grieve who knew You are safe in Your eternal presence. Let this truth comfort my soul. In Jesus' name, Amen.

Read More: John 10:27–29; Psalm 100:3; Isaiah 43:1; 1 Corinthians 6:19–20; Revelation 14:13

Thirty-Five

Light Trouble, Eternal Glory

> "For our present troubles are small and won't last very long. Yet they produce for us a glory that vastly outweighs them and will last forever." —2 Corinthians 4:17 (NLT)

Horatio Spafford, a successful 19th-century lawyer, lost his four daughters in a shipwreck. In his grief, he penned the hymn "It Is Well with My Soul." His words weren't denial—they were faith anchored in the hope of eternal glory beyond sorrow.[36]

Paul's words are striking, especially to those navigating the weight of sorrow. He doesn't minimize our troubles by calling them *"small."* Rather, he reframes them in light of eternity. When seen through the lens of heaven, even the most crushing grief cannot compare to the glory that awaits us in Christ.

This isn't a call to suppress grief or pretend everything is okay. It's an invitation to see our pain in its proper perspective.

Grief feels endless in the moment, but God promises it won't last forever. The losses we endure are producing something—something eternal. There's a weight of glory being formed that far surpasses the heaviness of sorrow.

This truth doesn't erase grief, but it gives it purpose. It encourages us to endure not because we're strong, but because God is using our trials to shape us for eternal life with Him. Heaven isn't just the absence of suffering—it is the fulfillment of God's promise to redeem every tear.

Practical Application:

Write down a grief or sorrow you're carrying. Then write next to it: "This won't last forever." Ask God to help you see your current pain through the eyes of eternity.

Reflection:

How does the promise of eternal glory bring hope into your present grief?

Prayer:

God, thank You for reminding me that what I'm facing now won't last forever. Help me to view my pain through Your eternal lens. Strengthen me to trust that every tear, every ache, is producing a future joy beyond imagination. In Jesus' name, Amen.

Read More: Romans 8:18; Revelation 21:4; Psalm 30:5; 2 Timothy 2:12; 1 Peter 1:6–7

Thirty-Six

Eyes on the Unseen

"So we don't look at the troubles we can see now; rather, we fix our gaze on things that cannot be seen. For the things we see now will soon be gone, but the things we cannot see will last forever." —2 Corinthians 4:18 (NLT)

In the 1952 Olympics, swimmer Florence Chadwick attempted to cross from Catalina Island to the California coast. After 15 hours in icy fog, she quit—just one mile from shore. Later she said, "If I could have seen the land, I might have made it."[37] Her story reminds us that what we fix our eyes on determines how long we endure.

Grief has a way of consuming our sight. It narrows our focus to what's missing, broken, or painful. But Paul encourages us to shift our gaze, not to deny reality but to anchor ourselves in something deeper. The troubles we see now, as overwhelming as they feel, are temporary. But the unseen things—God's presence, His promises, eternal life—are forever.

Fixing our eyes on what is unseen doesn't mean ignoring pain. It means looking through the pain toward a greater truth. Faith is not blind optimism; it's clarity of eternal vision. It's choosing to trust that beyond this heartbreak is a Savior who sees, knows, and is preparing something better.

Loss reminds us of the fleeting nature of life. But Paul says this fleeting nature is exactly why we shouldn't base our hope on what we see. What's eternal—God's love, His promise of resurrection, and reunion with loved ones—is not seen with physical eyes, but with the eyes of faith.

Practical Application:

Each time you feel overwhelmed by your loss today, pause and say aloud: "This is temporary, but God's promises are eternal." Let this truth reframe your grief.

Reflection:

What "unseen" truths from God's Word are helping you endure your current season of grief?

Prayer:

Lord, help me to fix my eyes not on the pain I feel, but on the hope You've promised. Strengthen my faith to see beyond this moment into eternity. Thank You that what I'm going through is not forever—but You are. In Jesus' name, Amen.

Read More: Hebrews 11:1; Colossians 3:1–2; Romans 8:24–25; Isaiah 40:31; John 14:1–3

Thirty-Seven

We Do Not Grieve Without Hope

> "We want you to know what will happen to the believers who have died so you will not grieve like people who have no hope. For since we believe that Jesus died and was raised to life again, we also believe that when Jesus returns, God will bring back with him the believers who have died." —1 Thessalonians 4:13–14 (NLT)

When Pastor Levi Lusko lost his five-year-old daughter, Lenya, to an asthma attack, his world was shattered. Yet he clung to the promise of resurrection, writing in Through the Eyes of a Lion, "Grief is not the end of the story for those who know Jesus."[38] The pain remained—but now it had purpose.

Grief is a sacred part of the human experience, even for believers. The early church faced painful losses just like we do today. Paul's letter to the Thessalonians acknowledges their sorrow but offers a powerful distinction: Christian grief is infused with hope.

This hope is not denial or detachment—it's deeply rooted in the resurrection of Jesus. Just as He rose from the dead, so will all who belong to Him. Paul reminds us that our loved ones who died in Christ are not gone forever. We will see them again.

Hope doesn't erase grief. It redefines it. It allows us to cry, but not to collapse. It allows us to mourn, but not to despair. We grieve—but not as those without hope. That's the power of the gospel in our sorrow: we have a promise of reunion, restoration, and resurrection.

Practical Application:

Write down the name of a loved one you've lost. Besides their name, write "Not forgotten. Not gone forever." Thank God for the hope of reunion through Christ, and ask Him to comfort you with this truth daily.

Reflection:

How does the promise of resurrection shape your view of loss and eternity?

Prayer:

Father, thank You for the hope I have in Jesus. I still hurt, and I still grieve, but I know this pain is not the end. Remind me that because Jesus rose from the dead, death is not final. Fill my heart with Your comfort and my soul with the joy of reunion to come. In Jesus' name, Amen.

Read More: John 11:25–26; Romans 6:5; Revelation 21:4; 1 Corinthians 15:51–57; Psalm 116:15

Thirty-Eight

Comforted By the Coming of the Lord

> "For the Lord Himself will come down from heaven with a commanding shout ... First, Christians who have died will rise from their graves. Then ... we who are still alive and remain on the earth will be caught up in the clouds to meet the Lord in the air. Then we will be with the Lord forever. So encourage each other with these words." —1 Thessalonians 4:16–18 (NLT)

After the funeral of Christian singer TobyMac's son, Truett, fans noticed a recurring phrase in his posts: "See you at the dawn." It was a quiet yet confident expression of hope—faith that death isn't the end but the beginning of reunion through Christ.[39]

Facing persecution and loss, the early believers longed for hope. Paul reminded them that Jesus would return, the dead in Christ would rise, and all believers would be reunited with the Lord forever.

This passage paints a breathtaking picture of eternity—our stories, and those of our loved ones in Christ, are not finished. Death's separation will be undone, every loss redeemed, and we will dwell forever in the glorious presence of Jesus.

When Paul says, *"encourage each other with these words,"* it's not a suggestion but a holy command to be spoken over our grief, shared in our sorrow, and whispered in hospital rooms and graveyards—reminding us, even in our sorrow, that hope still lives.

Practical Application:

When you feel the weight of loss, read this Scripture aloud. Let the truth of Christ's return and the promise of reunion strengthen you. Consider sending this passage to someone grieving today.

Reflection:

How does the promise of Christ's return help you face the pain of separation and the reality of death?

Prayer:

Jesus, thank You for the promise that You will return. Thank You that death will not win, and that those who have gone before us in faith will rise again. Comfort my heart with the hope of reunion and the assurance of being with You forever. Please help me share that hope with others. Amen.

Read More: Philippians 3:20–21; John 14:3; Isaiah 25:8; 2 Corinthians 5:1–2; Titus 2:13

Thirty-Nine

The Gain of Eternal Life

"For to me, living means living for Christ, and dying is even better." —Philippians 1:21 (NLT)

When missionary Jim Elliot prepared for service in Ecuador, he famously wrote in his journal, "He is no fool who gives what he cannot keep to gain that which he cannot lose."[40] His words gained new weight when he was martyred in 1956. Though his earthly life was cut short, his testimony has continued to inspire generations with the truth that life in Christ—even in death—is never wasted.

Paul's declaration in Philippians 1:21 is both bold and deeply comforting. He isn't dismissing the pain of death but rather redefining it through the lens of Christ. For the believer, life is an opportunity to serve Christ, and death is a doorway to be with Him forever. It's not a loss; it's a gain.

This eternal perspective profoundly alters how we perceive grief. Though we mourn the absence of loved ones, we grieve with hope because they are not gone forever—they are home. For those who die in Christ, death is not defeat but promotion to glory. And for those of us who remain, our purpose is to live every day for Jesus until we, too, are called home.

This doesn't mean the sting of loss disappears. It means we don't face it alone or without hope. When Paul said *"dying is even better,"* he was anchoring our grief to eternity. Jesus has conquered the grave, and that changes everything.

Practical Application:

Spend time reflecting on what "living for Christ" means for you today. How does the reality of eternal life reshape your priorities, your grief, and your relationships?

Reflection:

How does the assurance of gaining Christ in death bring comfort in your journey through grief and loss?

Prayer:

Lord Jesus, thank You that my life has meaning in You and that death is not the end. When grief clouds my heart, remind me that You have secured eternity for me and those I love who've trusted You. Help me live with purpose and die with peace. In Jesus' name, Amen.

Read More: 2 Timothy 4:6–8; John 11:25–26; 1 Corinthians 15:55–57; Revelation 14:13; Romans 14:8

Forty

A Life Well Finished

"The time of my death is near. I have fought the good fight, I have finished the race, and I have remained faithful. And now the prize awaits me—the crown of righteousness, which the Lord, the righteous Judge, will give me on the day of his return. And the prize is not just for me but for all who eagerly look forward to his appearing." —2 Timothy 4:6–8 (NLT)

Missionary Amy Carmichael served in India for over 55 years without furlough. Near life's end, bedridden and in pain, she kept writing letters of encouragement. She once wrote, "We have eternity to celebrate the victories, but only a few hours before sunset to win them." [41] Her life reminds us that faithfulness leaves a lasting fragrance of hope—even in death.

As Paul neared the end of his life, he faced death with peace, not fear. He had fought well, finished his race, and kept the faith—knowing a reward awaited him beyond this life.

His words remind us that death is not defeat. For believers, it marks the start of eternal reward and rest. Our loved ones in Christ have not lived in vain; they now wear the *"crown of righteousness."* Though we grieve, we also give thanks for their faithful example—and press on to finish our own race with the same hope, that we too, will receive our reward, on that faithful day.

Practical Application:

Write down one way your loved one faithfully did the Lord's work in their daily life. Let it inspire you to keep running your race with the same kind of faith and endurance.

Reflection:

What legacy of faith has your loved one left behind, and how can you honor it in your own walk with Christ?

Prayer:

Lord, thank You for the lives of those who have faithfully followed You to the very end. Help me to live with eternity in view—to fight the good fight, finish my race, and remain faithful. May their example spur me on, and may Your promise of reward comfort me in my grief. In Jesus' name, Amen.

Read More: Hebrews 12:1–2; Philippians 1:21; Revelation 2:10; 1 Corinthians 9:24–25; John 14:1–3

my notes

my notes

Endnotes

1. C.S. Lewis, *A Grief Observed* (New York: HarperOne, 2001), 1.

2. Nancy Guthrie, *Holding on to Hope: A Pathway through Suffering to the Heart of God* (Tyndale House, 2002).

3. Jason Hanna, Darran Simon, and Ralph Ellis, "Harvey aftermath: Houston hit with more flooding," *CNN*, August 30, 2017.

4. Kay Warren, "Finding God in the Midst of Tragedy," *Focus on the Family Broadcast*, accessed March 10, 2023.

5. Nancy Guthrie, *Hearing Jesus Speak into Your Sorrow* (Wheaton, IL: Tyndale House, 2009), 28–30.

6. Horatio G. Spafford, "It Is Well with My Soul." Written in 1873; Mark A. Noll, *A History of Christianity in the United States and Canada* (Grand Rapids: Eerdmans, 1992), 384.

7. "When Paradise was lost to wildfire, these Californians built it back," *The Times* (UK), February 10, 2025.

8. Mandisa Hundley, *Out of the Dark: My Journey Through the Shadows to Find God's Joy* (Colorado Springs: K-LOVE Books, 2022), 87–90.

9. Corrie ten Boom, *Tramp for the Lord* (Bantam Books, 1976), 83.

10. TobyMac, personal reflections and music following the death of his son. See Life After Loss by Christian Post, 2020.

11. Based on survivor testimony from CNN's post-earthquake coverage, January 2010.

12. Michelle Black, *Sacrifice: A Gold Star Widow's Fight for the Truth* (New York: G.P. Putnam's Sons, 2021).

13.

14. TobyMac, "The 700 Club Interview." [Video] TobyMac, Overcoming Loss Through Faith, *CBN*, 2020.

15. BBC News. "Thai Cave Rescue: One Year On," World-Asia 48864401, July 2019.

16. Michelle Boorstein, "A Year of Grief and Faith," *The Washington Post*, December 2020.

17. Kay Warren, *Choose Joy: Because Happiness Isn't Enough* (Grand Rapids: Revell, 2020), 142.

18. Kent Brantly, and David Thomas, *Called for Life: How Loving Our Neighbor Led Us into the Heart of the Ebola Epidemic*. (WaterBrook, 2015).

19. Brendan McDonough and Stephan Talty, *My Lost Brothers: The Untold Story by the Yarnell Hill Fire's Lone Survivor* (New York: Hachette Books, 2016).

20. Amanda Kloots, *Live Your Life: My Story of Loving and Losing Nick Cordero* (Harper, 2021).

21. Samantha Field, "Rachel Held Evans' Memorial Was the Gospel," *Rewire News Group*, June 4, 2019.

22. Kay Warren, "God, Grief, and Grace," *Saddleback Church Interview*, Watch-Media Library, accessed July 2025.

23. Steven Curtis Chapman, *Between Heaven and the Real World* (Revell, 2017).

24. Quoted in Daniel Darling, *The Characters of Easter: The Villains, Heroes, Cowards, and Crooks Who Witnessed History's Biggest Miracle* (Chicago: Moody Publishers, 2021), 147.

25. Chris Quilala, *Split the Sky* (Jesus Culture Music, 2016), album interviews and testimonies shared via Jesus Culture Podcast and media appearances.

26. Kay Warren, *Choose Joy: Because Happiness Isn't Enough* (Grand Rapids, MI: Revell, 2012), 153.

27. Kay Warren, *Sacred Privilege: Your Life and Ministry as a Pastor's Wife*. Revell, 2017.

28. Lisa Harper, *Life: From Broken to Beautiful* (Nelson Books, 2017).

29. David Gonzalez, "Haiti, After the Earthquake," *The New York Times*, January 15, 2010.

30. Philip Yancey and Paul Brand, *The Gift of Pain: Why We Hurt and What We Can Do About It* (Grand Rapids: Zondervan, 1997).

31. Kay Warren, *Choose Joy: Because Happiness Isn't Enough* (Grand Rapids: Revell, 2012), 104.

32. Jim Cymbala, "Because He Lives" Easter Service Message, Brooklyn Tabernacle Online Worship Service, April 12, 2020. Accessed via YouTube livestream and Brooklyn Tabernacle website.

33. Randy Alcorn, *Heaven* (Carol Stream, IL: Tyndale House Publishers, 2004), 10.

34. Amy Carmichael, *Candles in the Dark* (Fort Washington, PA: Christian Literature Crusade, 1981), 23

35. Elisabeth Elliot, *Suffering Is Never for Nothing* (Nashville: B&H Books, 2019), 15.

36. Philip P. Bliss, "It Is Well with My Soul," lyrics by Horatio G. Spafford, 1873; For biographical background, see Kenneth W. Osbeck, *101 Hymn Stories* (Grand Rapids, MI: Kregel Publications, 1982), 124–126.

37. Florence Chadwick, quoted in *The Speaker's Quote Book*, by Roy B. Zuck (Grand Rapids, MI: Kregel Publications, 1997), 98.

38. Levi Lusko, *Through the Eyes of a Lion: Facing Impossible Pain, Finding Incredible Power* (Nashville: Thomas Nelson, 2015), 12.

39. After the 2019 death of his son, Truett, Christian artist TobyMac often wrote, "See you at the dawn," a phrase expressing his hope in Christ and eternal life. (TobyMac, Instagram post, October 24, 2019)

40. Jim Elliot, journal entry, October 28, 1949, quoted in Elisabeth Elliot, *Shadow of the Almighty: The Life and Testament of Jim Elliot* (New York: Harper & Row, 1958), 108.

41. Amy Carmichael, *Edges of His Ways: Selections for Daily Reading* (Fort Washington, PA: Christian Literature Crusade, 1955), 100.

Other Books By Mike Prah

You Are Unstoppable: Practical Principles for Overcoming Setbacks and Experiencing Breakthroughs

DISCOVER HOW TO OVERCOME life's obstacles. In *You Are Unstoppable*, Mike Prah shares empowering biblical truths, inspiring stories, and practical strategies to help you experience breakthrough and live with purpose. **Available in Hardcover, E-Book and Audiobook.**

Step into your calling—because with God, you are truly unstoppable!

You Are Unstoppable: Personal or Group Study Guide

THIS POWERFUL 10-SESSION COMPANION to *You Are Unstoppable* is designed to help individuals and small groups apply life-changing biblical principles for breakthrough. With reflection prompts and discussion questions, Mike Prah equips you to turn setbacks into success and live with confidence, purpose, and freedom. You are truly unstoppable!

7 Secrets of Leaders Who Last

7 SECRETS OF LEADERS WHO LAST equips pastors, ministry leaders, and servant-leaders to overcome the most common traps that derail leadership and embrace the habits that ensure longevity.

Packed with a practical message outline, key takeaways, group discussion guide, and a 14-day devotional, this resource will help you grow spiritually, lead effectively, and finish strong.

Whether you're leading a church, a ministry team, or a small group, this guide will inspire and equip you to serve with focus, humility, and endurance.

Skill Will Bring Success: Proven Principles for Living the Life of Your Dreams

ARE YOU PUTTING IN THE EFFORT BUT NOT SEEING RESULTS? IT MAYBE TIME TO SHARPEN YOUR EDGE. Skill Will Bring Success is a transformative guide rooted in Ecclesiastes 10:10—reminding us that effort alone isn't enough. Mike Prah unpacks biblical wisdom and real-life principles to help you develop the emotional, spiritual, and professional skills necessary for lasting success.

With clear teaching, practical tools, and a companion study guide, this book equips you to break through limitations, grow in wisdom, and live the life God intended for you. Skill will bring your success to life.

Skill Will Bring Success: Personal or Group Study Guide

SHARPEN YOUR EDGE. EMBRACE YOUR PURPOSE. LIVE THE LIFE GOD DESIGNED FOR YOU.

This 10-session companion to Skill Will Bring Success helps you apply the book's transformational principles for personal growth, mentorship, or group study. Each session features clear teaching summaries, Scripture-based questions, practical steps, and guided prayers to deepen your walk with God.

Through biblical wisdom and real-life leadership lessons, Mike Prah equips you to develop the skills needed for success in every area of life. Don't just work harder—grow wiser. With God's help, skill will bring success!

Connect with Mike Prah

INSPIRED BY WHAT YOU READ?

Check out the following resources for spiritual guidance and inspiration at www.mikeprah.com.

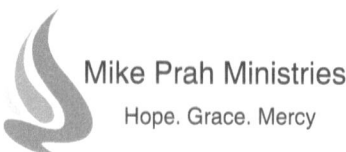

- Online store where you can buy books, merchandise, and special offers

- Book Excerpts

- First look at upcoming books

- Video Sermons, Podcasts, Blogs, Journals, and Articles

- Bible Study Lessons

For more information or to book Mike for a speaking engagement, please email info@mikeprah.com

Special Bulk Discounts and Custom Editions:

Most books authored by Mike Prah are available at special discounted rates for bulk purchases by churches, organizations, businesses, and individuals. Customized editions or book excerpts can also be created to meet the specific needs of your ministry, event, or audience. For more information or to inquire about a special order, please email info@mikeprah.com

www.ingramcontent.com/pod-product-compliance
Lightning Source LLC
Chambersburg PA
CBHW030446100526
44580CB00001B/3